VIRGINIA TEST PREP

Practice Test Book

SOL Math

Grade 4

ISBN 978-1482727487

CONTENTS

INTRODUCTION
For Parents, Teachers, and Tutors

About the Book

This practice test book contains three complete SOL Mathematics tests. The tests are just like the tests given by the state. Each test contains the same question types and styles, tests the same skills, and has the same length as the state test. If students can master the tests in this book, they will be prepared and ready to master the real SOL Mathematics test.

Taking the Test

Each test contains multiple-choice questions and questions that mimic the new technology-enhanced questions used on the state test. Students should answer the multiple-choice questions by filling in the circle of their answer choice in the test book. For the technology-enhanced questions, students should follow the instructions given with the question.

Timing the Test

Just like the real SOL Mathematics test, each practice test is divided into two sections. When taking the real SOL Mathematics test, students may complete both sections on the same day, or may complete each section on two consecutive days. If both sections are completed on the same day, students are given a break of at least 15 minutes between the two sections.

Students are given as much time as they need, but are expected to complete each section in about 60 minutes. It is not essential to time the test, but it is good preparation to ensure that students can complete each section in about 60 minutes.

Use of Calculators

Students are not allowed to use a calculator on Section 1 of each test. Students may use a calculator on Section 2 of each test.

TECHNOLOGY-ENHANCED QUESTIONS
For Parents, Teachers, and Tutors

The real SOL Mathematics test will include four types of technology-enhanced questions. These types are described below.

Fill-in-the-Blank Questions

Students type in letters, numbers, or symbols. These questions usually contain a blank box for students to type their answers into.

Drag and Drop Questions

Students move one or more draggers to drop zones on the screen. Draggers could be words, numbers, shapes, equations, or other elements. For examples, students may be asked to place all the rectangles in one drop zone, or may be asked to drag numbers to place them in order from lowest to highest.

Hot Spot Questions

Students select one or more hot spot zones. These hot spot zones are usually part of a chart, graph, or illustration. For example, students may select a point on a number line, a point on a coordinate plane, or a point on a shape. Students may also be asked to answer fraction questions by selecting shapes or parts of a shape to shade them.

Bar Graph or Histogram

Students complete a bar graph or histogram by creating a bar or column with the correct height or length.

This practice test book contains questions with similar formats to the technology-enhanced questions. They mimic the same processes that students will use to answer these questions online. These questions will help students become familiar with the formats of the technology-enhanced questions.

SOL MATHEMATICS

GRADE 4

PRACTICE TEST 1

SECTION 1

Instructions

Read each question carefully. For each multiple-choice question, fill in the circle for the correct answer. For other types of questions, follow the instructions given.

You may **not** use a calculator on this section of the test.

1 A company has 29 salespersons. Each salesperson works about 38 hours each week. About how many hours do all the salespeople work in all?

Ⓐ   70

Ⓑ   600

Ⓒ   900

Ⓓ   1,200

2 Joel bought a notepad for $1.25 and a pen for $1.65. How much money did Joel spend in all?

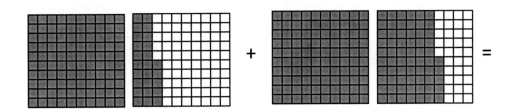

Ⓐ $2.70

Ⓑ $2.80

Ⓒ $2.90

Ⓓ $3.00

3 The table below shows the cost of food at a diner.

Drinks		Meals	
Small milkshake	$1.80	Plain hamburger	$3.50
Large milkshake	$2.00	Chicken burger	$4.20
Small soda	$1.10	Hotdog	$2.60
Large soda	$1.50	Meatball sub	$3.10
Fruit juice	$1.90	Quiche	$2.10

Lisa bought 2 different items and spent exactly $4.00. Circle the two items that Lisa bought.

Small milkshake	Plain hamburger
Large milkshake	Chicken burger
Small soda	Hotdog
Large soda	Meatball sub
Fruit juice	Quiche

4   The table below shows the entry cost for a museum.

Adult	$10 per person
Child	$8 per person
Family (2 adults and 2 children)	$30 per family

How much would a family of 2 adults and 2 children save by buying a family ticket instead of individual tickets?

Ⓐ $2

Ⓑ $6

Ⓒ $8

Ⓓ $10

5   Maria is reading a book with 286 pages. She has read 38 pages. Which is the best estimate of how many pages Maria has left to read?

Ⓐ   240

Ⓑ   250

Ⓒ   260

Ⓓ   270

6 A box of beads contains 2,000 beads. Chang buys 40 boxes of beads. How many beads did Chang buy?

Ⓐ 50

Ⓑ 500

Ⓒ 8,000

Ⓓ 80,000

7 A car traveled 52 miles in 1 hour. About how long would it take the car to travel 265 miles?

Ⓐ 3 hours

Ⓑ 4 hours

Ⓒ 5 hours

Ⓓ 6 hours

8 Jenna buys 8 packets of letter paper. Each packet contains 16 sheets of paper. How many sheets of paper did Jenna buy in all? Write your answer on the line below.

_____

9   Donna has $8.45. She spends $3.75. How much money does Donna have left?

　　Ⓐ　$3.70

　　Ⓑ　$3.30

　　Ⓒ　$4.70

　　Ⓓ　$4.30

10   The table below shows the number of male and female students at Hill Street School.

Gender	Number
Male	2,629
Female	2,518

How many students go to the school in all? Write your answer on the line below.

_____

11 A pet shop sells fish for $3 each. The pet shop sold $96 worth of fish one day. How many fish did the pet shop sell that day?

Ⓐ 32

Ⓑ 36

Ⓒ 48

Ⓓ 288

12 Which number is a factor of 57?

Ⓐ 11

Ⓑ 13

Ⓒ 17

Ⓓ 19

13 Which number is a multiple of 6?

Ⓐ 3

Ⓑ 20

Ⓒ 36

Ⓓ 50

END OF SECTION 1

SOL MATHEMATICS

GRADE 4

PRACTICE TEST 1

SECTION 2

Instructions

Read each question carefully. For each multiple-choice question, fill in the circle for the correct answer. For other types of questions, follow the instructions given.

You may use a calculator on this section of the test.

14   A motorbike has a weight of 255 kilograms. What is the weight of the motorbike in grams?

    Ⓐ   2,550 grams

    Ⓑ   25,500 grams

    Ⓒ   255,000 grams

    Ⓓ   2,550,000 grams

15   Which number rounds to 18?

    Ⓐ   17.2

    Ⓑ   17.7

    Ⓒ   18.9

    Ⓓ   19.3

16 Which unit would be best to use to measure the length of a box of tissues?

    Ⓐ   Yards

    Ⓑ   Miles

    Ⓒ   Centimeters

    Ⓓ   Kilometers

17 What decimal is equivalent to the fraction $\frac{5}{8}$? Write your answer on the line below.

_____

18   Jayden wants to find the length of a paperclip. Which unit would Jayden be best to use?

- Ⓐ   Millimeters
- Ⓑ   Milligrams
- Ⓒ   Grams
- Ⓓ   Kilometers

19   Kenneth got on a train at 9:30 in the morning. He got off the train at 1:20 in the afternoon. How long was Kenneth on the train for? Write your answer on the lines below.

_____ hours _____ minutes

20 Which single transformation is represented in the models of the lightning bolts?

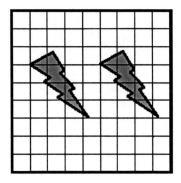

Ⓐ   Reflection

Ⓑ   Translation

Ⓒ   Rotation

Ⓓ   Dilation

21 Which of the following describes the rule for this pattern?

1, 3, 6, 8, 11, 13, 16

Ⓐ   Add 2, add 3

Ⓑ   Add 2, multiply by 2

Ⓒ   Multiply by 3, multiply by 2

Ⓓ   Multiply by 3, add 3

22   David filled the bucket below with water.

About how much water would it take to fill the bucket?

Ⓐ   5 milliliters

Ⓑ   5 pints

Ⓒ   5 liters

Ⓓ   5 quarts

23   Plot the decimal 1.75 on the number line below.

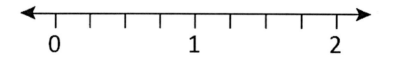

24   Which of the following diagrams shows a translation?

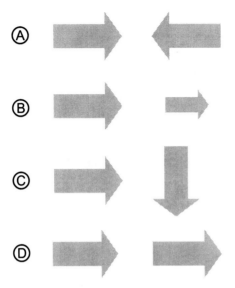

25   A pumpkin weighs 4 pounds. How many ounces does the pumpkin weigh?

Ⓐ   32 ounces

Ⓑ   40 ounces

Ⓒ   48 ounces

Ⓓ   64 ounces

26 The table below shows the population of 3 towns.

Town	Population
Franklin	18,725
Torine	24,214
Maxville	16,722

Which number sentence shows the best way to estimate how much greater the population of Torine is than Franklin?

Ⓐ   24,000 – 16,000 = 8,000

Ⓑ   24,000 – 17,000 = 7,000

Ⓒ   24,000 – 18,000 = 6,000

Ⓓ   24,000 – 19,000 = 5,000

27 Erin is sorting 65 quarters into piles. She puts the quarters in piles of 5.

Complete the number sentence below to show how many piles of quarters Erin has.

_____ ÷ _____ = _____

28 A movie made $5,256,374 in its first weekend. What does the 2 in this number represent?

    Ⓐ   Two thousand

    Ⓑ   Twenty thousand

    Ⓒ   Two hundred thousand

    Ⓓ   Two million

29 The graph shows how far four students travel to school.

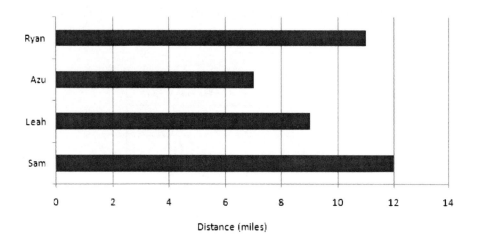

Distance (miles)

How much farther does Ryan travel than Azu?

    Ⓐ   7 miles

    Ⓑ   11 miles

    Ⓒ   4 miles

    Ⓓ   3 miles

30 Shade the model below to show $1\frac{6}{10}$.

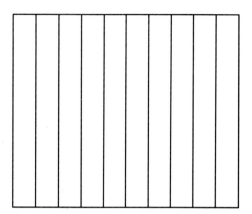 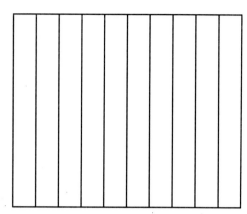

31 The table below shows the amount Davis spent on phone calls for four different months.

Month	Amount
April	$9.22
May	$9.09
June	$9.18
July	$9.05

In which month did Davis spend the least on phone calls?

Ⓐ April

Ⓑ May

Ⓒ June

Ⓓ July

32 Which single transformation could have changed Figure F to Figure G?

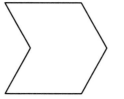

Figure F   Figure G

Ⓐ   Rotation

Ⓑ   Reflection

Ⓒ   Translation

Ⓓ   Not here

33 The sizes of the drill bits in a set are measured in inches. Which size drill bit is greater than $\frac{1}{2}$ inch?

Ⓐ $\frac{3}{8}$ inch

Ⓑ $\frac{7}{16}$ inch

Ⓒ $\frac{1}{8}$ inch

Ⓓ $\frac{9}{16}$ inch

34 What is the rule to find the value of a term in the sequence below?

Position, *n*	Value of Term
1	3
2	4
3	5
4	6
5	7

Ⓐ 2*n*

Ⓑ 3*n*

Ⓒ *n* + 2

Ⓓ *n* + 3

35 Which word describes the whole shape below?

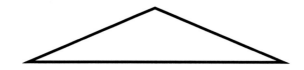

Ⓐ Ray

Ⓑ Point

Ⓒ Angle

Ⓓ Polygon

36 Look at the line segments shown below.

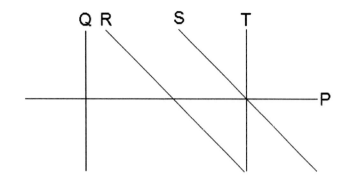

Which two line segments are parallel?

Ⓐ Line segment P and line segment Q

Ⓑ Line segment R and line segment S

Ⓒ Line segment Q and line segment R

Ⓓ Line segment S and line segment T

37 Which of these is the best estimate of the length of a baseball bat?

Ⓐ 3 inches

Ⓑ 3 feet

Ⓒ 3 millimeters

Ⓓ 3 centimeters

38 There are 40,260 people watching a baseball game. Which of these is another way to write 40,260?

    Ⓐ   4 + 2 + 6

    Ⓑ   40 + 2 + 60

    Ⓒ   40,000 + 200 + 6

    Ⓓ   40,000 + 200 + 60

39 The model below is shaded to show $2\frac{4}{10}$.

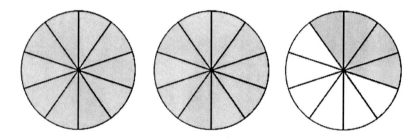

Which decimal does the model represent?

    Ⓐ   2.04

    Ⓑ   2.4

    Ⓒ   0.24

    Ⓓ   20.4

40   Which of the following is another way to write the numeral 600,032?

   Ⓐ   Six hundred thousand and thirty-two

   Ⓑ   Six million and thirty-two

   Ⓒ   Six hundred and thirty-two

   Ⓓ   Six thousand and thirty-two

41   The wingspan of the butterfly is 6.7 centimeters.

What is the wingspan of the butterfly in millimeters?

   Ⓐ   0.067 mm

   Ⓑ   0.67 mm

   Ⓒ   67 mm

   Ⓓ   670 mm

42 Mary has 2 red balloons and 3 green balloons. She chooses one balloon at random. What is the probability she chooses a red balloon?

  Ⓐ   2 out of 3

  Ⓑ   2 out of 5

  Ⓒ   3 out of 5

  Ⓓ   1 out of 2

43 What is 83,460 rounded to the nearest hundred?

  Ⓐ   83,000

  Ⓑ   84,000

  Ⓒ   83,400

  Ⓓ   83,500

44 Which pair of numbers completes the equation below?

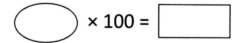

  Ⓐ   (60) and [6,000]

  Ⓑ   (60) and [60,000]

  Ⓒ   (6) and [60]

  Ⓓ   (6) and [6,000]

45 Troy recorded the number of sales he made each month.

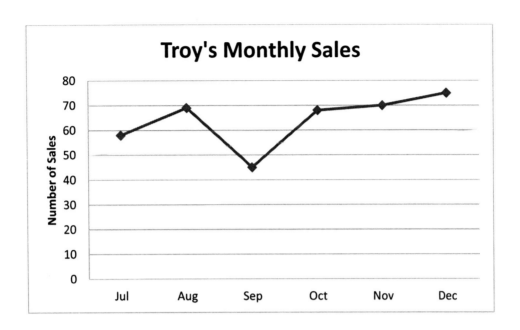

Between which two months did Troy's sales increase the most?

Ⓐ July to August

Ⓑ August to September

Ⓒ September to October

Ⓓ November to December

46 There are 40 blocks in a bag. The table shows the number of blocks of each color.

Color	Number
Red	12
Green	8
Yellow	16
Blue	4

Kathy selects a block at random. Which color block has a 3 in 10 chance of being selected?

Ⓐ   Red

Ⓑ   Green

Ⓒ   Yellow

Ⓓ   Blue

47   Which single transformation is represented below?

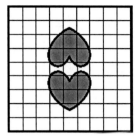

Ⓐ   Reflection

Ⓑ   Translation

Ⓒ   Rotation

Ⓓ   Not here

48   What is another way to write the fraction $\frac{9}{4}$?

Ⓐ $1\frac{1}{4}$

Ⓑ $1\frac{3}{4}$

Ⓒ $2\frac{1}{4}$

Ⓓ $2\frac{3}{4}$

49   Jackie made this table to show how much she received in tips on the four days that she worked.

Day	Amount
Monday	$32.55
Tuesday	$31.98
Thursday	$30.75
Friday	$32.09

On which day did Jackie earn the most in tips?

Ⓐ   Monday

Ⓑ   Tuesday

Ⓒ   Thursday

Ⓓ   Friday

50   If the pattern continues, which number will come next? Write your answer on the blank line.

6, 9, 12, 15, 18, 21, _____

END OF TEST

SOL MATHEMATICS

GRADE 4

PRACTICE TEST 2

SECTION 1

Instructions

Read each question carefully. For each multiple-choice question, fill in the circle for the correct answer. For other types of questions, follow the instructions given.

You may **not** use a calculator on this section of the test.

1 What are all the common factors of 10, 20, and 40? Circle all the common factors.

1   2   4   5   8   10   20   40

2 What is the product of 9 and 12? Write your answer on the line below.

_____

3 Ari is putting photos in an album. He can fit 6 photos on each page. He has 44 photos to place in the album. If he puts 6 photos on each page and the remainder on the last page, how many photos will be on the last page?

Ⓐ 1

Ⓑ 2

Ⓒ 3

Ⓓ 4

4   Mrs. Smyth has 82 colored pencils. She wants to divide them evenly between 8 people. How many whole pencils will each person receive? Write your answer on the line below.

_____

5   Sandy has $12.90. Marvin has $18.50. What is the total value of their money?

   Ⓐ $3.04

   Ⓑ $3.14

   Ⓒ $30.40

   Ⓓ $31.40

6   The table below shows the number of students in each grade at the David Hall School.

Grade	Number of Students
3	254
4	235
5	229

How many students are there in all? Write your answer on the line below.

_____

7   Mia is setting up tables for a party. Each table can seat 6 people. Mia needs to seat 36 people. Mia wants to find how many tables she will need. Write the correct sign in the box to show the correct number sentence to use.

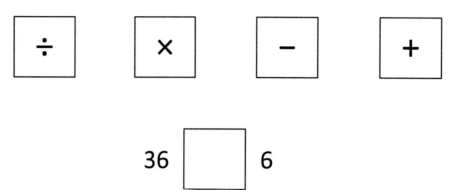

$$36 \;\boxed{}\; 6$$

8   Jed has 12 dimes, 18 nickels, and 42 pennies. What is the greatest common factor Jed can use to divide the coins into equal piles?

    Ⓐ   2

    Ⓑ   4

    Ⓒ   6

    Ⓓ   12

9 Vienna is buying gift cards. Each packet contains 12 gift cards. Vienna wants to buy 36 gift cards. Which of these can be used to find the number of packets of gift cards that Vienna should buy?

Ⓐ   36 x 12

Ⓑ   36 + 12

Ⓒ   36 ÷ 12

Ⓓ   36 – 12

10 Zoe has 90 small lollipops, 30 large lollipops, and 55 candies.

What is a common factor Zoe could use to divide the treats into equal groups?

Ⓐ   3

Ⓑ   5

Ⓒ   10

Ⓓ   15

11 A school cafeteria offered four Italian meal choices. The table below shows the number of meals served of each type.

Meal	Number Served
Pasta	151
Pizza	167
Salad	213
Risotto	117

Which is the best estimate of the total number of meals served?

Ⓐ 630

Ⓑ 650

Ⓒ 660

Ⓓ 670

12 Jay made 8 trays of 6 muffins each. He gave 12 muffins away. Which expression can be used to find how many muffins he had left?

Ⓐ $(8 \times 6) - 12$

Ⓑ $(8 \times 6) + 12$

Ⓒ $8 + 6 - 12$

Ⓓ $8 + 6 + 12$

13 A basket of 42 strawberries has a mass of 788 grams. Which is the most reasonable estimate of the mass of 1 strawberry?

Ⓐ 16 grams

Ⓑ 20 grams

Ⓒ 25 grams

Ⓓ 40 grams

END OF SECTION 1

SOL MATHEMATICS

GRADE 4

PRACTICE TEST 2

SECTION 2

Instructions

Read each question carefully. For each multiple-choice question, fill in the circle for the correct answer. For other types of questions, follow the instructions given.

You may use a calculator on this section of the test.

14 Which of these is the best estimate of the mass of a watermelon?

Ⓐ   5 ounces

Ⓑ   5 grams

Ⓒ   5 pounds

Ⓓ   5 milligrams

15 Shade the model below to represent 0.65.

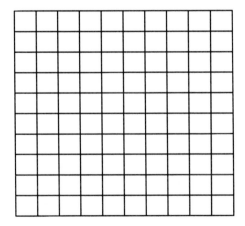

16 Sam has 15 DVDs in her bookcase. The table below shows the different types of DVDs Sam has in her bookcase.

Type of DVD	Number of DVDs
Action	3
Comedy	7
Drama	4
Science fiction	1

If Sam picks 1 DVD from the bookcase without looking, what is the probability that she will pick a comedy?

Ⓐ $\dfrac{7}{15}$

Ⓑ $\dfrac{4}{15}$

Ⓒ $\dfrac{3}{12}$

Ⓓ $\dfrac{7}{8}$

17 Each number that was put into the number machine below changed according to a rule.

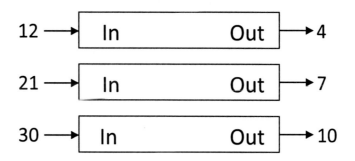

Which equation describes the rule for the number machine?

Ⓐ   Number in × 3 = number out

Ⓑ   Number in + 20 = number out

Ⓒ   Number in ÷ 3 = number out

Ⓓ   Number in − 8 = number out

18 Which polygon has 6 sides?

Ⓐ   Pentagon

Ⓑ   Square

Ⓒ   Hexagon

Ⓓ   Triangle

19   What decimal does the shaded model represent?

Write your answer on the line below.

_____

20   The shaded model below represents a fraction.

Which model below represents an equivalent fraction?

Ⓐ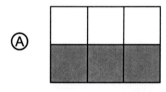

Ⓑ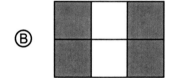

Ⓒ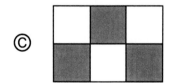

Ⓓ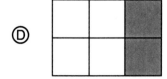

21 Karen made this table to show her monthly phone bills.

Month	Amount
April	$5.42
May	$5.39
June	$5.51
July	$5.27

Place the months in order from the lowest bill to the highest bill. Write the months on the lines below.

Lowest   _____

              _____

              _____

Highest   _____

22 Which digit is in the thousands place in the number 6,124,853?

Ⓐ   6

Ⓑ   1

Ⓒ   2

Ⓓ   4

23   Which decimal does the shaded model below represent?

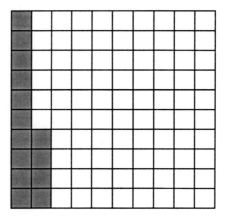

Ⓐ   1.4

Ⓑ   0.014

Ⓒ   0.14

Ⓓ   14.0

24   Which number has a 4 in the millions place?

Ⓐ   8,340,386

Ⓑ   5,468,950

Ⓒ   4,082,663

Ⓓ   8,934,159

25 The diagram below shows two sets of black and white stickers.

Which of the following compares the portion of black stickers in each set?

Ⓐ $\frac{8}{9} > \frac{2}{3}$

Ⓑ $\frac{8}{9} < \frac{2}{9}$

Ⓒ $\frac{2}{3} < \frac{1}{3}$

Ⓓ $\frac{1}{9} > \frac{6}{9}$

26   The grade 4 students at Diane's school are collecting cans for a food drive. The table below shows how many cans each class collected.

Class	Number of Cans
Miss Adams	36
Mr. Walsh	28
Mrs. Naroda	47

Which is the best way to estimate the number of cans collected in all?

Ⓐ   30 + 20 + 40 = ?

Ⓑ   30 + 30 + 40 = ?

Ⓒ   40 + 30 + 50 = ?

Ⓓ   40 + 30 + 40 = ?

27   Which measurement is equal to 12 pints?

Ⓐ   3 quarts

Ⓑ   6 quarts

Ⓒ   24 quarts

Ⓓ   48 quarts

28 Identify the place value for each digit in the number 234.15. Draw a line to match each digit with its place value.

1	hundreds
2	hundredths
3	ones
4	tens
5	tenths

29 If *n* is a number in the pattern, which rule can be used to find the next number in the pattern?

4, 6, 8, 10, 12, 14, 16, ...

Ⓐ $n + 2$

Ⓑ $n - 2$

Ⓒ $n + 4$

Ⓓ $n - 4$

30   What part of the model is shaded?

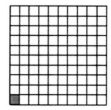

    Ⓐ   0.01

    Ⓑ   0.1

    Ⓒ   1

    Ⓓ   10

31   Which of these shapes has exactly one pair of perpendicular sides?

Ⓐ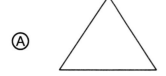

Ⓑ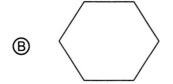

Ⓒ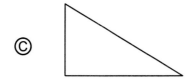

Ⓓ

32   Round 8.782 to the nearest tenth. Write your answer on the line below.

_____

33   Lloyd has 4 white shirts and 1 blue shirt. He chooses one shirt at random. What is the probability he chooses a blue shirt?

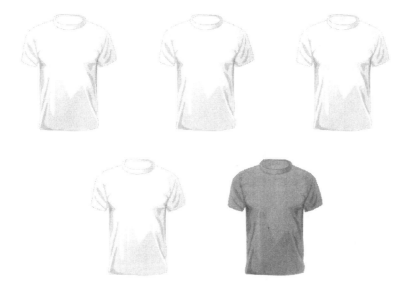

   Ⓐ   0.2

   Ⓑ   0.25

   Ⓒ   0.5

   Ⓓ   0.8

34 The graph below shows how long Jody studied each week day.

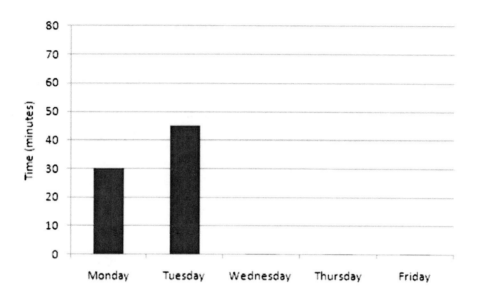

Jody studied for 55 minutes on Wednesday, 70 minutes on Thursday, and 35 minutes on Friday. Add three bars to the graph to show Jody's study time on Wednesday, Thursday, and Friday.

35 Which term describes each edge of the triangle?

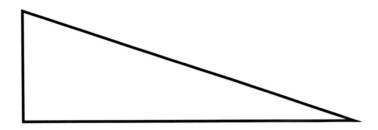

Ⓐ   Point

Ⓑ   Line segment

Ⓒ   Angle

Ⓓ   Endpoint

36 Madison used $1\frac{3}{4}$ cups of milk to make a milkshake. Which of the following is another way to write $1\frac{3}{4}$?

Ⓐ $\frac{4}{4}$

Ⓑ $\frac{13}{4}$

Ⓒ $\frac{7}{4}$

Ⓓ $\frac{12}{4}$

37   Andy was buying a used car. He had four cars in his price range to choose from. The four cars had the odometer readings listed below.

Car	Chrysler	Ford	Honda	Saturn
Reading (miles)	22,482	21,987	23,689	22,501

If Andy decided to buy the car with the second highest odometer reading, which car would be buy?

Ⓐ   Chrysler

Ⓑ   Ford

Ⓒ   Honda

Ⓓ   Saturn

38   Which number goes in the box to make the equation below true? Write your answer in the box below.

$$44 \div \boxed{} = 11$$

39 Which pair of figures shows a reflection?

Ⓐ

Ⓑ

Ⓒ

Ⓓ

40 Which model is shaded to show a fraction equivalent to $\frac{6}{10}$?

Ⓐ

Ⓑ

Ⓒ

Ⓓ

41 Jade made a pattern using marbles. The first four steps of the pattern are shown below.

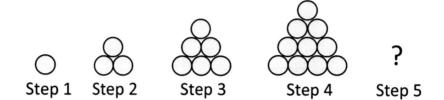

Step 1   Step 2   Step 3   Step 4   Step 5

If Jade continues the pattern, how many marbles will she need for Step 5?

Ⓐ 13

Ⓑ 14

Ⓒ 15

Ⓓ 16

42 Which single transformation is shown below?

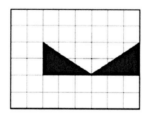

Ⓐ Translation

Ⓑ Reflection

Ⓒ Rotation

Ⓓ Not here

43   Which of these is the same as 3 × 6 × 2?

Ⓐ   3 × 2 × 6

Ⓑ   6 × 6 × 2

Ⓒ   3 + 6 + 2

Ⓓ   3 × 6 ÷ 2

44   Which pair of numbers best completes this table?

Number	Number × 10
850	8,500
3,501	35,010
19	190

Ⓐ

28	208

Ⓑ

365	36,500

Ⓒ

1,987	19,870

Ⓓ

6	600

45 The model below shows $2\frac{8}{100}$ shaded.

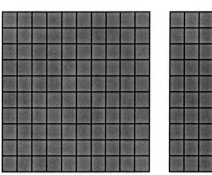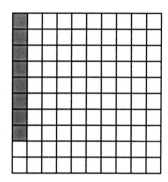

What decimal represents the shaded part of the model?

Ⓐ   2.8

Ⓑ   2.08

Ⓒ   200.8

Ⓓ   200.08

46 Joy started a hike at 1:50. It took Joy 2 hours and 25 minutes to finish the hike. What time did Joy finish the hike?

Ⓐ   3:35

Ⓑ   3:50

Ⓒ   4:05

Ⓓ   4:15

47   Ronald competed in a swimming race. All the students finished the race in between 42.5 seconds and 47.6 seconds. Which of the following could have been Ronald's time?

   Ⓐ   41.9 seconds

   Ⓑ   40.5 seconds

   Ⓒ   46.8 seconds

   Ⓓ   48.1 seconds

48   Which figure is shown below?

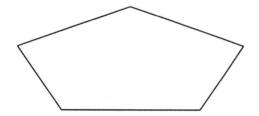

   Ⓐ   Pentagon

   Ⓑ   Hexagon

   Ⓒ   Octagon

   Ⓓ   Decagon

49 Which procedure can be used to find the next number in the sequence?

$$120, 60, 30, 15, \ldots$$

(A) Subtract 15 from the previous number

(B) Add 15 to the previous number

(C) Multiply the previous number by 2

(D) Divide the previous number by 2

50 Which of these is the best estimate of the mass of an apple?

(A) 100 milligrams

(B) 100 grams

(C) 100 kilograms

(D) 100 tons

END OF TEST

SOL MATHEMATICS

GRADE 4

PRACTICE TEST 3

SECTION 1

Instructions

Read each question carefully. For each multiple-choice question, fill in the circle for the correct answer. For other types of questions, follow the instructions given.

You may **not** use a calculator on this section of the test.

1   What are the common factors of 6, 9, and 15? Circle all the common factors.

1   2   3   5   6   9   15

2   Bruce is counting his quarters. He puts them in 35 piles of 5. How could you work out the total value of the quarters?

Ⓐ   Divide 35 by 5, and multiply the result by $0.25

Ⓑ   Multiply 35 by 5, and multiply the result by $0.25

Ⓒ   Divide 35 by 5, and divide the result by $0.25

Ⓓ   Multiply 35 by 5, and divide the result by $0.25

3 A bakery makes muffins in batches of 12. The bakery made 18 batches of muffins. Which is the best estimate of the number of muffins made?

Ⓐ 100

Ⓑ 400

Ⓒ 250

Ⓓ 200

4 A school divided its grade 4 students into 6 classes. There were exactly 26 students in each class. How many students were there in all? Write your answer on the line below.

_____

5   Katie saw the sign below at a fruit stand.

If Katie spent $6 on oranges, how many oranges would she get? Write your answer on the line below.

_____

6   The normal price of a CD player is $298. During a sale, the CD player was $45 less than the normal price. What was the sale price of the CD player?

Ⓐ $343

Ⓑ $333

Ⓒ $263

Ⓓ $253

7 Bagels are sold in packets of 4 or packets of 6. Kieran needs to buy exactly 32 bagels. Which set of packets could Kieran buy?

Ⓐ   2 packets of 4 bagels and 4 packets of 6 bagels

Ⓑ   3 packets of 4 bagels and 3 packets of 6 bagels

Ⓒ   4 packets of 4 bagels and 2 packets of 6 bagels

Ⓓ   5 packets of 4 bagels and 1 packet of 6 bagels

8 What is the product of 8 and 9?

Ⓐ   56

Ⓑ   64

Ⓒ   72

Ⓓ   81

9   A bakery ordered 60 cartons of eggs. There were 12 eggs in each carton. Which number sentence could be used to find *e*, the total number of eggs the bakery ordered?

Ⓐ   60 x 12 = *e*

Ⓑ   60 + 12 = *e*

Ⓒ   60 – 12 = *e*

Ⓓ   60 ÷ 12 = *e*

10   An array for the number 36 is shown below.

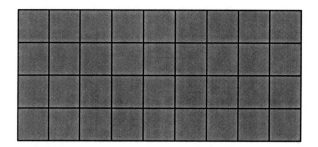

Which number is a factor of 36?

Ⓐ   9

Ⓑ   8

Ⓒ   5

Ⓓ   7

11   What is the least common multiple of 3, 4, and 8?

Ⓐ   12

Ⓑ   16

Ⓒ   24

Ⓓ   96

12   Donna bought a lollipop for $0.60 and a candy for $0.15 cents. How much change would Donna receive from $1?

Ⓐ $0.15

Ⓑ $0.25

Ⓒ $0.35

Ⓓ $0.75

13 Leanne added $\frac{1}{4}$ cup of milk and $\frac{3}{8}$ cup of water to a bowl. Which diagram is shaded to show how many cups of milk and water were in the bowl in all?

Ⓐ

Ⓑ

Ⓒ

Ⓓ

END OF SECTION 1

SOL MATHEMATICS

GRADE 4

PRACTICE TEST 3

SECTION 2

Instructions

Read each question carefully. For each multiple-choice question, fill in the circle for the correct answer. For other types of questions, follow the instructions given.

You may use a calculator on this section of the test.

14   Which figure below has exactly 4 angles?

Ⓐ

Ⓑ

Ⓒ

Ⓓ

15   Shade the model below to show $1\frac{7}{10}$.

16   Which number goes in the box to make the equation below true? Write your answer in the box below.

$$54 \div \boxed{} = 9$$

17 Which shaded model represents $\frac{5}{4}$?

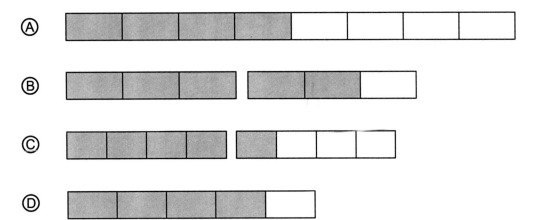

Ⓐ

Ⓑ

Ⓒ

Ⓓ

18 Lei jogs for the same number of minutes every day. The table shows how far she jogs in total after 1, 2, 3, and 4 days.

Number of Days	Number of Minutes Jogged
1	15
2	30
3	45
4	60

Based on the pattern in the table, how many minutes will Lei have jogged for after 7 days?

Ⓐ   75 minutes

Ⓑ   90 minutes

Ⓒ   105 minutes

Ⓓ   120 minutes

19   What is the most likely capacity of the cooking pot?

Ⓐ   2 cups

Ⓑ   2 pints

Ⓒ   2 quarts

Ⓓ   2 gallons

20   Which shaded model shows a fraction greater than $\frac{4}{5}$?

Ⓐ

Ⓑ

Ⓒ

Ⓓ

21   What is the number 457,869 rounded to the nearest ten thousand?

    Ⓐ   450,000

    Ⓑ   460,000

    Ⓒ   457,000

    Ⓓ   458,000

22   Which shape below is an octagon?

Ⓐ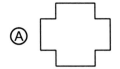

Ⓑ

Ⓒ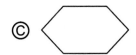

Ⓓ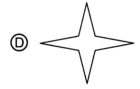

23 Which expression is the same as (8 + 2) + 5?

Ⓐ 8 – (2 + 5)

Ⓑ 8 + (5 + 2)

Ⓒ (8 + 2) – 5

Ⓓ (8 – 2) – 5

24 Which is the best estimate of the length of a football?

Ⓐ 10 inches

Ⓑ 10 millimeters

Ⓒ 10 meters

Ⓓ 10 yards

25 What decimal does the shaded model below represent?

Ⓐ 0.1

Ⓑ 0.2

Ⓒ 0.25

Ⓓ 0.5

26 Which measurement is the same as 80 ounces?

Ⓐ 5 pounds

Ⓑ 8 pounds

Ⓒ 20 pounds

Ⓓ 40 pounds

27   Which fraction does the shaded model below represent?

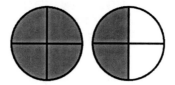

   Ⓐ $\dfrac{4}{6}$

   Ⓑ $\dfrac{6}{4}$

   Ⓒ $\dfrac{2}{4}$

   Ⓓ $\dfrac{1}{4}$

28   David filled the bucket below with water.

About how much water would it take to fill the bucket?

   Ⓐ   5 cups

   Ⓑ   5 pints

   Ⓒ   5 quarts

   Ⓓ   5 gallons

29 Each number in Set P is related in the same way to the number beside it in Set Q.

Set P	Set Q
2	8
6	12
8	14
10	16

When given a number in Set P, what is one way to find its related number in Set Q?

Ⓐ   Multiply by 4

Ⓑ   Multiply by 2

Ⓒ   Add 6

Ⓓ   Add 8

30 In which number sentence does the number 8 make the equation true?

Ⓐ $48 \div \square = 6$

Ⓑ $\square \div 6 = 48$

Ⓒ $48 \times 6 = \square$

Ⓓ $\square \times 48 = 6$

31 Circle all the figures below that have a right angle.

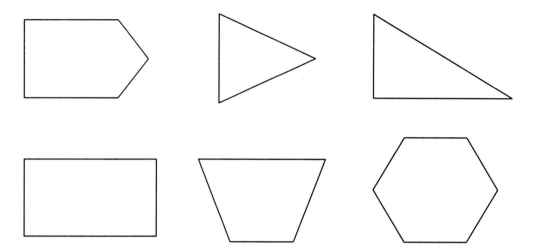

32 Which single transformation is shown below?

Ⓐ   Rotation

Ⓑ   Reflection

Ⓒ   Translation

Ⓓ   Not here

33 Circle each measurement that is the same as 3 yards.

6 feet   9 feet   12 feet

12 inches   24 inches   36 inches

34 A standard coin is tossed. What is the probability that the coin lands on either heads or tails?

Ⓐ   0

Ⓑ   0.25

Ⓒ   0.5

Ⓓ   1

35 The table below shows the number of meals a café served on four different days.

Monday	Tuesday	Wednesday	Thursday
1,487	1,510	1,461	1,469

Place the days in order from the least to the most number of meals served. Write the days on the lines below.

Least   _____

         _____

         _____

Most   _____

36 Which set of transformations could change the position of the triangle as shown below?

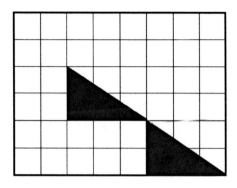

Ⓐ   Two translations

Ⓑ   A translation and a reflection

Ⓒ   A rotation and a translation

Ⓓ   Two rotations

37 The population of Greenville is 609,023. What does the 9 in this number represent?

Ⓐ   Nine thousand

Ⓑ   Ninety thousand

Ⓒ   Nine hundred thousand

Ⓓ   Ninety

38   Which number is less than 35.052?

    Ⓐ   35.009

    Ⓑ   35.061

    Ⓒ   35.101

    Ⓓ   35.077

39   Plot the decimal 3.8 on the number line below.

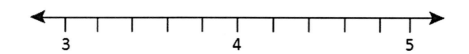

40   What part of the model is shaded?

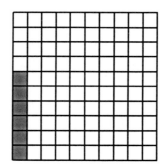

    Ⓐ   6.0

    Ⓑ   0.6

    Ⓒ   0.06

    Ⓓ   0.006

41   A park has a length of 60 feet. What is the length of the park in yards? Write your answer on the line below.

_____ yards

42   Which value of *p* makes the equation below true?

$$p \div 7 = 9$$

Ⓐ   49

Ⓑ   56

Ⓒ   63

Ⓓ   81

43   Which set of squares has exactly half of the squares shaded?

Ⓐ

Ⓑ

Ⓒ

Ⓓ

44 What is the rule to find the value of a term in the sequence below?

Position, n	Value of Term
1	3
2	6
3	9
4	12

Ⓐ $n \times 2$

Ⓑ $n \times 3$

Ⓒ $n + 2$

Ⓓ $n + 3$

45 Which statement is true?

Ⓐ 386 > 389

Ⓑ 412 > 450

Ⓒ 589 < 596

Ⓓ 611 < 610

46 The table below shows the total number of pieces of bread Aaron used to make peanut butter and jelly sandwiches.

Number of Sandwiches	Number of Pieces of Bread
2	6
4	12
8	24

Which of the following describes the relationship in the table?

Ⓐ   Number of sandwiches × 2 = number of pieces of bread

Ⓑ   Number of sandwiches × 3 = number of pieces of bread

Ⓒ   Number of sandwiches × 6 = number of pieces of bread

Ⓓ   Number of sandwiches × 8 = number of pieces of bread

47 How is the numeral 35.012 written in words?

Ⓐ   Thirty-five thousand and twelve

Ⓑ   Thirty-five and twelve thousandths

Ⓒ   Thirty-five and twelve hundredths

Ⓓ   Thirty-five and twelve

48 A recipe for a cake requires $1\frac{2}{3}$ cups of flour. Fill in the blank box below to show $1\frac{2}{3}$ as an improper fraction.

49 Which fraction model is equivalent to $\frac{2}{3}$?

Ⓐ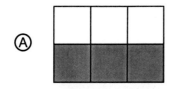

Ⓑ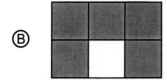

Ⓒ

Ⓓ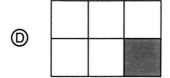

50 The table below shows the number of households in four different suburbs.

Suburb	Number of Households
Wellington	135,682
Ashton	179,441
Ellis	120,597
Mayfield	191,822

Which suburb has the most households?

Ⓐ   Wellington

Ⓑ   Ashton

Ⓒ   Ellis

Ⓓ   Mayfield

END OF TEST

ANSWER KEY

Tracking Student Progress

Use the answer key to score each practice test. After scoring each test, record the score in the Score Tracker at the back of the book.

As the student progresses, test scores will continue to improve as the student gains experience, knowledge, and confidence.

Topics and Math Skills

The SOL Mathematics test given by the state tests a specific set of skills and knowledge. The state divides these skills into six broad areas, or topics. These are:

- Number & Number Sense
- Computation & Estimation
- Measurement
- Geometry
- Probability & Statistics
- Patterns, Functions, and Algebra

The answer key identifies the topic for each question. Use the topics listed to identify general areas of strength and weakness. Then target revision and instruction accordingly.

The answer key also identifies the specific math skill that each question is testing. Use the skills listed to identify skills that the student is lacking. Then target revision and instruction accordingly.

PRACTICE TEST 1 ANSWER KEY

Question	Answer	Topic	Math Skill
1	D	Computation & Estimation	Estimate products of whole numbers
2	C	Computation & Estimation	Add and subtract with decimals
3	Fruit juice Quiche	Computation & Estimation	Add and subtract with decimals
4	B	Computation & Estimation	Solve multistep word problems
5	B	Computation & Estimation	Estimate differences of whole numbers
6	D	Computation & Estimation	Multiply whole numbers
7	C	Computation & Estimation	Estimate quotients of whole numbers
8	128	Computation & Estimation	Solve single-step word problems
9	C	Computation & Estimation	Add and subtract with decimals
10	5,147	Computation & Estimation	Add whole numbers
11	A	Computation & Estimation	Solve single-step word problems
12	D	Computation & Estimation	Identify factors of a number
13	C	Computation & Estimation	Identify multiples of a number
14	C	Measurement	Identify equivalent measurements of weight/mass
15	B	Number & Number Sense	Round decimals to a given place
16	C	Measurement	Estimate and measure length
17	0.625	Number & Number Sense	Write decimal and fraction equivalents
18	A	Measurement	Estimate and measure length
19	3 h 50 min	Measurement	Determine elapsed time
20	B	Geometry	Identify transformations
21	A	Patterns, Functions, Algebra	Recognize and describe patterns
22	C	Measurement	Estimate and measure liquid volume
23	point at 1.75	Number & Number Sense	Represent decimals on a number line
24	D	Geometry	Recognize the result of transformations
25	D	Measurement	Identify equivalent measurements of weight/mass
26	D	Number & Number Sense	Round whole numbers
27	$65 \div 5 = 13$	Patterns, Functions, Algebra	Understand and write equations
28	C	Number & Number Sense	Understand and identify place value
29	C	Probability & Statistics	Interpret data from graphs
30	See Below	Number & Number Sense	Represent mixed numbers
31	D	Number & Number Sense	Compare and order decimals
32	C	Geometry	Identify transformations
33	D	Number & Number Sense	Compare and order fractions
34	C	Patterns, Functions, Algebra	Recognize and describe patterns
35	D	Geometry	Understand what a polygon is
36	B	Geometry	Identify parallel lines
37	B	Measurement	Estimate and measure length
38	D	Number & Number Sense	Understand and apply place value
39	B	Number & Number Sense	Use models to convert from fractions to decimals

Question	Answer	Topic	Math Skill
40	A	Number & Number Sense	Read and write whole numbers
41	C	Measurement	Identify equivalent measurements of length
42	B	Probability & Statistics	Find the likelihood of an event
43	D	Number & Number Sense	Round whole numbers to a given place
44	A	Patterns, Functions, Algebra	Understand and write equations
45	C	Probability & Statistics	Interpret data from graphs
46	A	Probability & Statistics	Find the likelihood of an event
47	A	Geometry	Identify transformations
48	C	Number & Number Sense	Represent equivalent fractions
49	A	Number & Number Sense	Compare and order decimals
50	24	Patterns, Functions, Algebra	Identify and extend patterns

Q30.

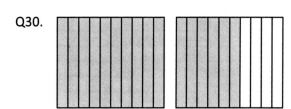

PRACTICE TEST 2 ANSWER KEY

Question	Answer	Topic	Math Skill
1	1, 2, 5, 10	Computation & Estimation	Identify common factors
2	108	Computation & Estimation	Multiply whole numbers
3	B	Computation & Estimation	Divide whole numbers with remainders
4	10	Computation & Estimation	Divide whole numbers with remainders
5	D	Computation & Estimation	Add and subtract with decimals
6	718	Computation & Estimation	Add whole numbers
7	÷	Computation & Estimation	Solve single-step word problems
8	C	Computation & Estimation	Find the greatest common factor of a number set
9	C	Computation & Estimation	Solve single-step word problems
10	B	Computation & Estimation	Identify common factors
11	B	Computation & Estimation	Estimate sums of whole numbers
12	A	Computation & Estimation	Solve multistep word problems
13	B	Computation & Estimation	Estimate quotients of whole numbers
14	C	Measurement	Estimate and measure weight/mass
15	See Below	Number & Number Sense	Represent decimals
16	A	Probability & Statistics	Represent probability as a fraction
17	C	Patterns, Functions, Algebra	Recognize and describe patterns
18	C	Geometry	Identify polygons
19	4.75	Number & Number Sense	Use models to convert from fractions to decimals
20	D	Number & Number Sense	Represent equivalent fractions
21	July, May, April, June	Number & Number Sense	Compare and order decimals
22	D	Number & Number Sense	Understand and identify place value
23	C	Number & Number Sense	Identify decimals from a model
24	C	Number & Number Sense	Understand and identify place value
25	A	Number & Number Sense	Compare and order fractions
26	C	Number & Number Sense	Round whole numbers
27	B	Measurement	Identify equivalent measurements of liquid volume
28	See Below	Number & Number Sense	Understand and identify place value
29	A	Patterns, Functions, Algebra	Recognize and describe patterns
30	A	Number & Number Sense	Identify decimals from a model
31	C	Geometry	Identify perpendicular lines
32	8.8	Number & Number Sense	Round decimals to a given place
33	A	Probability & Statistics	Represent probability as a decimal
34	See Below	Probability & Statistics	Display data in a graph
35	B	Geometry	Identify line segments
36	C	Number & Number Sense	Represent equivalent fractions
37	D	Number & Number Sense	Compare and order whole numbers
38	4	Patterns, Functions, Algebra	Understand and write equations
39	C	Geometry	Recognize the result of transformations

Question	Answer	Topic	Math Skill
40	D	Number & Number Sense	Represent equivalent fractions
41	C	Patterns, Functions, Algebra	Identify and extend patterns
42	B	Geometry	Identify transformations
43	A	Patterns, Functions, Algebra	Understand the associative property
44	C	Patterns, Functions, Algebra	Identify and extend patterns
45	B	Number & Number Sense	Use models to convert from fractions to decimals
46	D	Measurement	Determine elapsed time
47	C	Number & Number Sense	Compare and order decimals
48	A	Geometry	Identify polygons
49	D	Patterns, Functions, Algebra	Recognize and describe patterns
50	B	Measurement	Estimate and measure weight/mass

Q15.

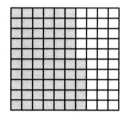

Q28.

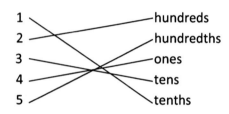

Q34.

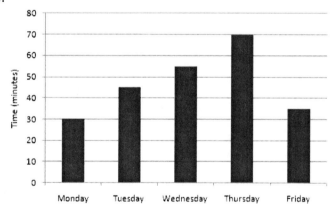

PRACTICE TEST 3 ANSWER KEY

Question	Answer	Topic	Math Skill
1	1, 3	Computation & Estimation	Identify common factors
2	B	Computation & Estimation	Solve multistep word problems
3	D	Computation & Estimation	Estimate products of whole numbers
4	156	Computation & Estimation	Multiply whole numbers
5	24	Computation & Estimation	Solve single-step word problems
6	D	Computation & Estimation	Subtract whole numbers
7	A	Computation & Estimation	Solve multistep word problems
8	C	Computation & Estimation	Multiply whole numbers
9	A	Computation & Estimation	Solve single-step word problems
10	A	Computation & Estimation	Identify factors of a number
11	C	Computation & Estimation	Find the least common multiple of a number set
12	B	Computation & Estimation	Add and subtract with decimals
13	D	Computation & Estimation	Add and subtract with fractions
14	A	Geometry	Identify angles
15	See Below	Number & Number Sense	Represent mixed numbers
16	6	Patterns, Functions, Algebra	Understand and write equations
17	C	Number & Number Sense	Represent mixed numbers
18	C	Patterns, Functions, Algebra	Identify and extend patterns
19	D	Measurement	Estimate and measure liquid volume
20	D	Number & Number Sense	Compare and order fractions
21	B	Number & Number Sense	Round whole numbers to a given place
22	D	Geometry	Identify polygons
23	B	Patterns, Functions, Algebra	Understand the associative property
24	A	Measurement	Estimate and measure length
25	D	Number & Number Sense	Use models to convert from fractions to decimals
26	A	Measurement	Identify equivalent measurements of weight/mass
27	B	Number & Number Sense	Represent equivalent fractions
28	D	Measurement	Estimate and measure liquid volume
29	C	Patterns, Functions, Algebra	Recognize and describe patterns
30	A	Patterns, Functions, Algebra	Understand and write equations
31	See Below	Geometry	Identify angles
32	C	Geometry	Identify transformations
33	9 feet 36 inches	Measurement	Identify equivalent measurements of length
34	D	Probability & Statistics	Represent probability as a number from 0 to 1
35	Wed, Thur, Mon, Tue	Number & Number Sense	Compare and order whole numbers
36	A	Geometry	Identify transformations
37	A	Number & Number Sense	Understand and identify place value
38	A	Number & Number Sense	Compare and order decimals
39	point at 3.8	Number & Number Sense	Represent decimals on a number line

Question	Answer	Topic	Math Skill
40	C	Number & Number Sense	Identify decimals from a model
41	20	Measurement	Identify equivalent measurements of length
42	C	Patterns, Functions, Algebra	Understand and write equations
43	A	Number & Number Sense	Represent fractions
44	B	Patterns, Functions, Algebra	Recognize and describe patterns
45	C	Number & Number Sense	Compare and order whole numbers
46	B	Patterns, Functions, Algebra	Recognize and describe patterns
47	B	Number & Number Sense	Read and write decimals
48	5	Number & Number Sense	Represent mixed numbers
49	C	Number & Number Sense	Represent equivalent fractions
50	D	Number & Number Sense	Compare and order whole numbers

Q15.

Q31.

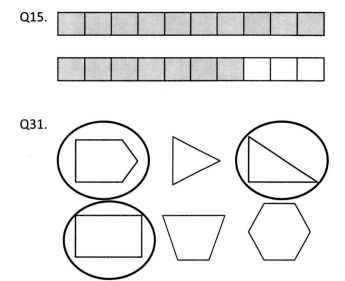

SCORE TRACKER

Test	Score
Practice Test 1	/50
Practice Test 2	/50
Practice Test 3	/50

VIRGINIA READING TEST PREP

For reading test prep, get the Virginia Test Prep Practice Test Book. It contains 6 reading mini-tests, focused vocabulary quizzes, plus a full-length SOL Reading practice test.

CPSIA information can be obtained at www.ICGtesting.com
Printed in the USA
BVOW06s1812070714

358382BV00002B/4/P